I Swear He Was Laughing

Poems About Dogs (Mostly) Who Only THINK They Are People, But Aren't, So Can't Read This Book, So Will You Please Read It for Them?

---

by Dean Blehert

Illustrations by Pam Coulter Blehert

Words & Pictures Press
Tustin, CA

This book is dedicated to G.I., whose name might have meant Government Issue, Gastrointestinal or Good Indicators, but, in fact, meant Gross Income for reasons that grew increasingly obscure as he became for us so entirely himself, G.I.

Copyright © 1996 by Dean Blehert

All rights reserved. No part of this book may be reproduced in any form or by any electronic or mechanical means including information storage and retrieval systems without permission in writing from the publisher, except by a reviewer, who may quote brief passages in a review.

Designed by Maggy Graham. Published by Words & Pictures Press, 18002 Irvine Blvd., Suite 200, Tustin, CA 92780, 714-544-7282.

ISBN No. 0-9644857-4-5
Library of Congress Catalog Card Number 96-60835

Introduction

Most of the poems in this book were previously printed in my "poetry letter," *Deanotations*, which, for nearly 12 years, has gone out every two months to a few hundred subscribers — each issue, like this book, containing my poems with my wife's drawings. Several readers suggested I make a book out of the dog poems. (That's a GOOD reader!)

Why all these poems about dogs? Perhaps because Pam and I have no children — or no OTHER children. Perhaps because, even more than children, dogs are such pure, revealing models of the human condition, each emotion turned on full volume, each moment heightened. Perhaps because they understand so much — wanting to console us when we're down, becoming furry cheerleaders when we're up — and yet understand NOTHING — not even when one swats them and screams at them over and over!

Perhaps because they are so with us . . . and then they are gone, leaving our poor little cat to sponge up all our unused attention. (She manages it — and demands more.)

I love dogs for all the trite reasons, their enthusiasm, sweetness, awkwardness, grace, etc., and also because at times when my own "rightness" was too rigid to allow for the existence of other people with inner lives as rich and important as my own, a dog pretending NOT to be a person would sneak into my rightness and shatter it. As I say in a long poem not included in this volume:

> I sit near the window reading,
> hardly aware of the dog asleep
> on his couch across the room.
> He stretches, lifts his head,
> scratches his chin with a few fast
> rhythmic swipes of a paw, then
> looks at me, and it astonishes me
> to think that he is here with me,
> has been with me all day, being
> whatever he is just as you and I,
> all along, have been with each other,
> an idea that stirs me as if I were
> a baby bursting with giggles
> each time Momma pokes her head
> in view and goes "Peek-a-BOO!"

I Swear He Was Laughing

The dog sprawls on the couch
as if dead, head hanging off the edge,
paws bent limply in the air. If,
from across two rooms, I look at him
or even, sharply, <u>think</u> of him,
his tail twitches. If my attention
persists, tail thumps against the couch,
backwards-hanging head opens round, upside-down,
quizzical brown eyes that find me
and hold me while torso and legs
tentatively stretch themselves off the couch
and carry quick-talking tail
and homing head to where I sit,
where, if I don't reach, long tapered
muzzle nuzzles under my wrist
and wedges head beneath hand —
I could refuse it, but would that
be fair? I <u>called</u> him,
didn't I?

Cinderella

That little white mutt eyes me
all aquiver with interest.

Life calls from solidity to solidity,
promising the melting of solids
into free motion.

        O hope! hope!
goes little white mutt with every
pant and twitch of tail and tongue —
O hope! — that there will be play, that
some passing prince (or kid with a stick
to toss) will say:

"Little White Mutt, may I have
the honor of the next dance?"

        ❦

The dog has had enough cuddling
and uncoils off the bed.
I stare at my skin,
watching for any freckles
that move.

        ❦

When I've learned to feel joy
and sorrow more intense
than any man has known,
I can become a great poet or even a dog.

Consummation

Suddenly all nose, the dog
sniffs a frantic zig zag
toward invisible treasure:
Quick! There . . . there . . . Ah!
<u>Here's</u> the magic spot! And
Exactly dead center over it
squats
and shits.

You whimper at sight of another dog
half a block away — as if I'm tearing you
away from long-sought home.
But If I let you trot off to mingle
at a doggy doing, you sniff and circle each other,
warily, back-fur erect, then
you lope slowly back to me, head
slung low — disappointed? It must
have been an ancient pack you thought
you'd sighted, and a joy beyond words,
had you words, to streak like wind
through woods behind a real leader
(not a tall stiff slow poke like me),
with fresh-killed bloody haunch for the
swiftest, not the chemically preserved,
soyed and breaded "nuggets" I dish up.
I'd help you find your pack if I knew
where to look. I too once had
another home (and when the wind

is right, it seems to be just beyond
those trees . . .). We will make do.
WATCH it! Car! Stay by me! Good boy.

❧

The dog, who leaves messages in urine,
likes to watch me flush the toilet,
admiring our high tech: He thinks
I'm making a long-distance call.

❧

Putting One's Best Foot In It

I got up naked to get a pen
to write poems before sleep,
stepped in a pile of soft dog shit,
tracked it tip-toe to the paper towels,
cleaned floor (gagging) and foot,
yelled at and swatted a cowed dog

and now I'm in bed with a pen
about as ready to write poetry
as I'll ever be.

❧

Late autumn — all the squirrels are fat.
Don't bark so, my friend — soon
they'll need that energy.

The dog lopes ahead,
starts as the grass hurls two black
birds into a tree.

I walk to the door. From the drowzing
armchairs, a double eruption
of eager dog. Quickly I close the door
behind just me. How can I explain
that I must hurry over a blur of
concrete, deaf to the lively yarns spun
by a billion unsniffed scents?

You Sly Dog, You!

A black mutt puppy tries to adopt those children.
The girls chase him away
with sticks (lightly) and girlish-rough voices,
he retreats, squats in the grass
watching them play, then ambles up again.
They scold and chase him away.

They will lose sight of him eventually, and later
that girl who smiles when she shoos him
will wonder what became of him and feel
a twinge of sorrow when she hears of Dog Pounds,
a ghost of guilt when she sees a run-over dog.

As for the mutt, he enjoys his game.
If he were a man, he'd stand on the corner,
whistling at chicks, pathetic, charming.

As for me, a quiet adult on his park bench,
I can't whistle, but if I were a dog,
I would make the little girl who yells so harsh
and laughs so sweet chase <u>me</u>.

A Good Licking

If, having ventured
one tentative lick at the tip
of my nose, he was not
shoved away, he'd set to it
industriously: long hot sweeping tongue
would stroke my lips (soon sealed) and nose
again and again,

while far up the long black snout,
as if aiming at me over a rifle barrel,
his dark shiny eyes —
glassier than usual —
met mine.

I let him do this to me
(not as often as he wanted it)
because I thought it let him return
our love for him. When at last
he'd subside, I'd say "Thank you",
which would stir another briefer flurry
of tonguing.

Or maybe he craved the salt on my skin.

Early on I learned to keep my mouth shut —
that muscular tongue could probe as well as caress.
Where does a dog learn to French-kiss?

Afterwards I'd wash my face, but his tongue
had probably washed it better than soap could.

He wanted to lick Pam's face too, but she always
held him off and NO'd him, his tongue flicking
vainly once, twice, thrice before her face
in diminishing dabs — ick! mustn't touch! —
an offering refused. That must be why
sometimes when she expects me to kiss her,
I lick her cheek or nose:
I do it for you, old mutt —

Or maybe I'm salt deficient.

As we walk away,
The dog's barks become fewer
In the winter air.

Curb Your Doggerel

You know that you can't have your treat
Until you've done your business.
Not on the path! Please be discreet
And spare our neighbors' queasiness.
Don't gaze up at me from my feet
With sweet big-brown-eyed quizziness!
Just do your duty quick and neat
Or we'll be here till Chrisimess!

"Tic . . . tic . . . tic . . . " (The dog by our bed scratches.) "Quiet!" I yell. Silence . . . "Tic . . . tic . . . tic . . . " (He can't help ticking — he's a watch dog.)

If this dog attacks,
I could kick him there or else . . .
Just walk, Samurai.

❦

Growing fatter, we admire more
our sleek, long-shanked black mutt,
as if stretching ourselves skinny
in a funhouse mirror, for people
resemble their pets: In him is our hope
(fat chance!) that this blubber
is temporary, not touching our essence.

❦

Out of the pond,
collie shakes loose in the sun
a silver cloud.

❦

Starting From Scratch

Red Brandy whimpers, squirms, rubs her rump
against my knees to be scratched.
Black Charo licks my bare ticklish toes.
Bimbi, the shepherd, thrusts her torn frisby
into my lap to be tossed (if I can grab it
before she snaps it up again). At last,
I shoo them away so I can write.

Strange, for what more can I want?
Is not love love? What can I put
into a poem that I cannot give to them
through my hands and voice, pouring it out
as fast as it can fill me up?

Maybe they are too easy:
One wants a game. And, no,
love is <u>not</u> love. I scratch the dogs;
I realize who I am before a mirror
and smile; I have sex with my wife,
then lie beside her, seeing,
slowly drifting downstream, a river
of places I have never been;

and I write poems to anyone who ever has
or will learn to understand words,
then walk among strangers on teeming streets,
buoyantly, as at a reunion with the old gang.

With my trusty dogs at my side,
I go forth to create a culture.
A little nuzzling and scratching must be
how we reward each other
for a hard day's trailblazing.
Love endures only as the fun of doing
something else together. Something else
must always be a reach for some other realms
of love, which, reached, must become
the fun of doing something else together.
Love for love's sake, like the slow,
meaty-warm lick of a dog's tongue
across one's face, is too true to endure
or be endured for long.

The poet reads; outside a dog howls:
mutual critics.

In the park, from a distance,
I say hello to a girl, who says
hello back, not that we want
to know each other, but it's the least
we can do while our dogs
sniff each other's behinds.

Dogs sweat through their tongues.
I'm being licked on the cheek
by a dog's armpit.

The dog beats her tail
on the floor: WHACK WHACK WHACK.
I wish I could do that.

"Here's your food," I say.
"I love you!" says the dog.
"Sit," I say.
"I love you!" says the dog.
"Come here," I say.
"I love you!" says the dog.
I feel loved, yet misunderstood.

Poof! Snow-showered,
the dog jumps, eyes me. It wasn't me!
The tree did it!

Just for a second, he looked
so natural there, the dog
curled up on the good couch
where he's not permitted,
but as my gaze brushed past him,
he lowered his, and I remembered.

As when walking the dog
I carry a pooper-scooper,
so, when walking alone,
I carry a pen and notebook,
in case a poem happens
on public property.

&

German Shepherd rages at me from a yard.
(Someone shut the mutt up!) Then
a lady going the other way, peroxided,
preserved, immaculate in tennis whites
(she <u>belongs</u> on this street
of wide sloping lawns), in passing,
glares at me (must be my half-grown
beard). A moment later — hark! I hear
the dog — good boy! — barking at <u>her</u>!

&

BAD body! BAD BAD body! Naughty! Get away
from me! You're a <u>Bad Body</u> —
FAT body! OLD body! Stop begging —
you HAD your supper.   Get away from me!
Bad Bad body.

&

A dog barks out back;
nearby an answer; far off
another; miles away . . .

&

Dog Days

The dog overturns the garbage.
I swat the dog.
The dog is properly propitiative.
I feel mean and futile.
The dog overturns the garbage.
I swat the dog.
The dog is properly propitiative.
I feel mean and futile.
(I write this poem.
The dog overturns the garbage . . . .)

&

We take the dogs with us when we jog.
As soon as they see us in our running shorts,
those limp rumpled blankets on the rug
explode into infinite puppydom.
Behind us in the car — pant!
pant! pant! The rear-view mirror is full
of long pink squirming tongues. Out
of the car quick to the grass — look
at this! Look at that! Over here! No —
here! Sniff! Sniff! Sniff! Sniff!
(Piss Piss) Sniff! Dogs can talk
so clearly here. Around the earnest line
of our jogging, they embroider
rococo mazes of romping curves.
Secure in what they feel to be
the rock-firm stability of our serious
universe (whence the bags and cans
of dog food flow ceaselessly), they
weave about us the only stable universe
(we lived in it as children), giving us
all they imagine we give them — the
endlessly interesting play of wind
and sun on tall grass, the shock

of thicket exploding into bird or Rabbit,
wondering where each path leads,
what's down that creek? . . . We stolidly
exhaust ourselves and fall on the grass;
they trot over and trot away and trot over and trot away,
tireless. I would like to speak
to these excited beings as I speak to
you and have them understand. I guess
that's why one has children. But
children grow up (I guess because
they want to understand) and forget
to know what's worth understanding
unless their dogs remind them.

Old dog wanders off; I haul him back, as time
gets slippery.

Carpe Canine
Or: Hark! Hark! The Dogs Do Barf!

Now what's that dog chewing?
Surely something he shouldn't.
From a can or a cat box,
Whether bone or soft puddin' it,
This Pollyannish dog
Always finds something good in it.
He gobbles it down,
Then plays dumb — Hollywoodn't
Do it better, as if saying
"Something wrong? I wonder whodoneit?"
I'll find out what he scarfed
When, tomorrow, all chewed-on, it
is barfed on our carpet
And I put my foot in it.

Walking past —
BARK! BARK! BARK! BARK! BARK!
Don't think it hasn't.

The cats and dogs know
it's man's world: They go
On tiptoe.

Old dog romps, licking and sniffing, over the
first snow, mingled messes of autumn smells
blanketed with cool, crisp, unstoried
freshness, against which the first pristine
piss is a pungent miracle of clarity, blood-rich and
ice-keen, a masterpiece of doggie art.

※

The dogs of third world countries
are not like ours: preoccupied
with covering their noon shadows and
being covered by other shadows, smart
about cars, caring nothing about
people nor wanting to be one of them,
barely noticing them, stepping slowly
through vacant lots like survivors
of too many bombings.

※

Wanted Distractions

As I picked lint from the couch
in search of ideas for poems,
one dog came and plopped his long chin
on my notebook to have his head scratched.
Then the shepherd dropped her grubby rubber frog
at my feet and barked (to get me to throw it).

Now they've gone about their doggy business,
and, again, I'm of no use to anyone
unless I can find something to say worth saying.

Hot, humid night — like a refrigerator surge,
the dog's panting.

Another NO DOGS
ALLOWED sign. Mine would lift
a leg and piss on it.

❧

"Down, Tolstoy! Down!" — at the reading,
a lady with a Russian wolfhound.

❧

Tonight I move out. Also in, don't
forget in. Someday the empty room
where tonight I'll unload a few boxes
of just my things will be a place
I'll say goodbye to gently, as if
scratching a dog behind the ear, saying
"No, you stay here. It's OK, it's
allright, that's a good boy."

❧

A dog and a stick . . . the dog wins!

❧

Dog on Braided Rug

They spend so much of life napping —
because we give them so few games to play —
that they have learned to sublimate
lost motion into semblances of sleep:

The splayed rear paws, triple-arched
torso, tucked-in tail, tucked-under snout,
crumpled ears and twisting forelegs tell the tale;

This braided rug is a magic place where sleep
is a field of tall grass, where — a black streak! —
he runs excited circles around us, where he knows
we are near.

Dog On Braided Rug, II

Now I understand why he settles down
so carefully, with nuzzlings, sniffs, and three
methodical turns round the spot before he flops
on the braided rug, just missing its bullseye —

for who would not select with care
a jumping-off place for this free-fall
limbo of loose limbs angled crazily

athwart the rug, what we humans tame
by putting it in beds behind locked doors
and calling it "sleep".

This rug is where he anchors to our presence
before spinning off into ear-twitching, soft-
puppy-whimper dreams —
in technicolor? Perhaps not,
but what these homey colors are to us,
the smell of our presence and of the crumbs
of munched milkbone and old fur-fluffs
(become warp and weft of this old rug)
are to his most perilous dreams.

A long walk with the dog —
a three-pile walk.

Like Cats and Dogs

Grampa had this joke — he'd reach for my nose with a growl, yell "GOT IT!" and snatch away his hand, then, beaming, show me his fist with the tip of the thumb exposed between index and middle finger — "See — there it is!"

I'd loved my dog for years, but felt almost faint with tenderness the first time he snatched at me with his snout — in play — growling, and clacked his teeth together just a hair short of my nose-tip. Then, to be sure I got the joke, he licked me — and laughed. (It's a look, no haha, just a tongue-heavy bright-eyed panting.)

Years later we had a feisty black & white kitten smaller than my hand, but each night as I lay in bed, he'd attack any exposed hand — again and again, clasping it with all four needled paws, ready to sink in his teeth if not dislodged. Tired of tossing him away, I began to wear an old kitchen glove and let him tear away at it each night until he tired of the game. But the first leg out of bed each morning found itself encumbered by a bit of black and white fuzz clinging to the ankle.

This was one tough kitten. It even attacked the dog, leapt at him from around chairs, from above, from behind. Oh oh, I thought, and pulled the 60-pound dog away, lest one swipe of his paw destroy the kitten.

One morning Pam called me into the hall to see dog and kitten fighting — not fighting, but rolling around roughhousing each other. Or rather, the cat may have been fighting (later both the dog's punctured ears needed lancing and stitching and were crooked ever after), but the dog was playing. He'd open his crocodile jaws around the entire head and shoulders of his foe, then snap them shut just missing, not touching a single kitten whisker. The kitten clung to his tail, his legs (one at a time), made chirpy snarls, hissed, scratched, and that dog rolled, squirmed, tail-thumped, snapped and growled and laughed like mad, I swear he was laughing,

But you may say, well, they LOOK like they're laughing, it's that long toothy jaw, that dab of pink tongue, but dogs can't laugh. OK, but I hope no one ever has YOU for a grampa.

Old poodle can't see
or hear much. He wobbles up
to my leg, leans there,
wanting love, also to rub
runny eyes on my clean pants.

A Crossing

The dog crosses the road. I say
"Come back here". The dog doesn't seem
to hear me. A car comes. NOW
the dog starts to cross back to me.
I yell STAY! The dog doesn't seem
to hear. The car halts for the dog,
who, eventually, toddles almost up to me,

then, sensing something's wrong,
stops just beyond my reach, head down,
eyes peering up at mine, then away
from beneath worried brows.
COME HERE! I say. The dog doesn't seem
to hear. YOU COME HERE **NOW** I scream.
The dog moves a hesitant step forward,

I lunge, catch his bright red collar and
(for his own good) swat his shoulder hard

and again . . . . He ducks, cringes,
looks up at me, blinking, looks away.

I feel bad. I wonder if I should never
have children. Where did I go wrong?

☙

Physics Lesson

I knock on a door, wondering
which state of life will greet me;
stony adults bravely fracturing
to make muscles move lips politely;
shy liquid thaw of a child's smile
reaching out in wavelets to lap at me;
hot gas of dog exploding every which way;
or, from the eyes of a cat,
freezing us both, a vacuum.

☙

We oversleep. Two cats and two dogs
gather about the bed, sober-eyed,
anxious, like doctors consulting.

☙

A dog trots by, like all dogs,
knowing, somehow, to look at
my eyes.

>>>

Hard to sit on the grass
when the dog is with me. He always
tries to lick my face. And I always
say "Back!" or "Down!" — which, in
dog, translates to "No, Honey,
I'm just not in the mood tonight."

>>>

From bathroom to bed . . . oops! Tripped
on a black furry speed bump.

>>>

You are not home yet (the clock ticks
as hard as it can), and you are not
home yet and you continue to be
not home yet in spite of all a clock
can do.

The cat and the dogs are tired of waiting
for you. The kitchen table is tired
of waiting for you. The ceiling is
particularly tired of waiting for you.
Soon the night, after long waiting,
will have to leave without having
seen you. I am not waiting
for you. I am just here, where
eventually you will be. I sit up
with the table, the dogs, the ceilings,
the night, politely keeping them
company on their vigil.
Where are you?

Each with a white fluff of poodle
pulling on a leash, they spot each other
100 yards apart. Each lifts her poodle
into her arms, and, warily,
they approach each other
with poodles drawn.

"Men" says the shrink "are animals."
They are not. Even animals aren't
animals, not MERE animals. Even
psychiatrists aren't animals. At least,
no dog or cat of MY acquaintance
would admit to being
a psychiatrist.

L.A. night. Three stray dogs
pant up, sniff me, trot off,
thinking, "Where's his car?"

&

At the house — the dogs
glad to see me. Don't they know
I'm out of favor?

&

It must be breeding — old Brandy,
who never hunted anything except bones
in the kitchen trash bag, spots quail,
gallops off, half points, looks back at me,
bewildered — aren't I going to
shoot something? (Perhaps with my
notebook? My pen?)

&

Riddle: Why did the dog cross the road
without permission?
Because he's a goddamned idiot
and he'll never learn!

&

We have cats, dogs and
urine smell in every season
of the haiku.

In Manhattan the people used to roam free,
but now rarely are the tame ones
allowed out on the streets at night
unless led on a leash
by a large dog.

"Yip! Yip! Yip!"
goes the little dog,
each muscle, each hair convulsing
in his need to tell everyone
that a stranger is at the door. "Shush!"
they tell him, "It's OK." But he won't
shush; he knows his duty! So they
drag him from the room, poor prophet.

Hard to express how much
someone at the door changes the universe.
To express this, we have
poems and dogs.

&

Don't look at me that way, you dumb dog!
I explained I'll feed you right away,
as soon as I finish . . . Oh, all right!
But it's not fair, your not being able
to understand!

&

The dog peers up at me, dabbing at air
with his vivid tongue. "I'll bet you want
another bone," I say, and my friend,
across the table behind a pile of my poems, says
"Not now — I've read enough today."

&

Irish setter tiptoes
through the poetry reading,
won't stop to be patted.

&

Walking Beside You

Walking ahead of you
(it is hard for me to walk at your pace),
I worry: What if an alien craft
were to beam you up, just you.
I'd be walking along, turn back—
you'd be gone
forever.

So I slow down to walk beside you.
Still, with a narrow beam,
they could pick off you alone,

so I put my hand on your shoulder,
but maybe they'd take you
and just my hand,

and you'd worry,
what happened to the rest of me,
did I bleed to death,
or did the beam cauterize my stump?—

you'd never be certain.

Would you save my hand?
Would they let you remember me?

I'd never be certain.

Our old dog would be barking like mad,
snarling at the empty sky.
He'd be inconsolable.

They'd put me away, too—
In jail if I had no explanation,
or in an asylum if I tried
to tell the truth.

How nice to walk along,
(the dog nuzzling our hands
then falling behind
to sniff at the grass)
kicking the autumn leaves,
beside you.

Far down the mountainside I see a tiny patch
of grass where tiny bodies hurl frisbies back and
forth, three ignored dogs weaving a pattern
of excited busyness around their legs.

≈

Gold cocker spaniel looks at me from the lawn,
lies there, doesn't bark. I look back and write.
These are strong considerations, that he's a dog,
that I'm writing — hard to change. Must be
someone else's ideas, not ours, for it's hard
to change your ideas only if they're someone else's.
It would resolve elegantly if it were his idea
that I'm a poet and mine that he's a dog — a simple
swap. Nothing has changed, so I guess that's not it . . .
why am I scratching myself?

≈

Halloween
two runty ghosts bob down the lawn—
O! A white poodle.

≈

When the dogs crowd my knees to lick and be
    scratched,
they are such cute good-old corny critters . . .
but who or what gazes at me
out of this cozy Norman Rockwell scene
with sober Rembrandt eyes?

❦

The dogs plop down on the floor against my feet,
and, like obscene phone-callers,
do nothing to show their love except
breathe hard and fast.

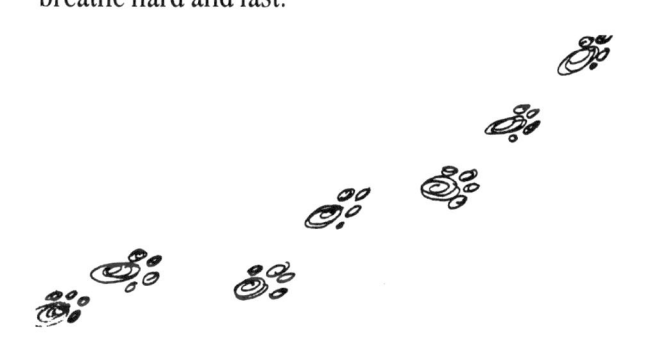

The dog trots ahead.
Paws touch sidewalk with a pat
patter pat like leaves.

❦

Ill-bred dog! I've never met you before,
yet you bound into my lap,
committing forepaw upon forepaw.

❦

THUMP-pitpat THUMP-pitpat:
Through the house moves something six-legged:
Pam and the dog. Morning.

❦

Old dog paces,
paces, waiting for death . . .
or birth.

❦

Old black dog,
new bald patches at the elbows —
how Ivy League!

❦

The sign says "City Animal Shelter."
Auschwitz was perhaps a Jew shelter?

❦

The dog stands still, glassy eyed, hardly
there at all, as I wet and soap and rinse
and dry him. "There, all done . . ." —
wet paws up in my lap, quick tongue
in my face, then a romp of rampaging fur
fills the house.

The dog crawls up on the bed with me;
I let him stay: My nearness means
So much to him, so little to me.

Old dog limps now.
In sleep he stretches out, runs,
as in dreams I fly.

My ability to love gets dried up
by my crimes against love.
On days when wind-swept skies
nuzzled me and begged to be hugged,
I have preferred to be entirely upset
with the driver ahead of me for not
turning on the orange light. I have
insulted people for doing their jobs.
I have swatted dogs for not
understanding my anger with them. I have
been angry with women who loved me
for losing trifles or simply
liking the wrong music. It is
a crime, at least against myself,
to make myself blind and deaf and
untouchable in order to be right.

※

"It's alright! It's a friend! Shhh!
SHUT UP!!" Damned dog slinks away from the
front door, thoroughly bow-wow-beaten.

※

"Can I pet your dog?" "Sure."
The dog's gaze asks me
"What is this?"

&

"Good boy!" After 12 years
still magic words:
I get licked.

&

I walk past where the dog
Is stretched out on the couch —
Thump! Thump! Thump!
The Case of the Telltale Tail.

&

It's the beef-liver dog food. The
Ingredients feature (low on the list)
Beef, but higher up, "Meat by-products."
Ah! Lone Ranger, why didn't you tell me
That someday I'd have to feed my horsie
To my doggie!

Bleeping motherbleeping bleep-sucking dumb dog!
Can't you tell a carpet from a toilet?
Don't you EVER EVER do that again!
Not EVER EVER EVER EVER!" (Shoving her nose in it.)
Now she slinks about with long sideways looks.
Dumb dog. I invest my hard-earned cash
in dog food to fill her gullet,
and she deposits it as dog shit on my
rug. I hold onto this anger as if rage
were going out of style. Dumb shit dog.
Rage rage against the dying of the light.
Stupid dog.

It is good to know,
as I trudge along these streets,
that my passing brings such excitement
into the lives of so many
earnest dogs.

&

Polka-dots float in air,
dissolve into a snow drift —
a Dalmatian.

&

I, too, feel bad about the world dying.
It's like our dog aging so much faster
than we do.

&

My Good Dog

My good dog grows old.
His mild clouded eyes are lidded by chafed black leather.
I fear he will die without first becoming fully human
or something. I fear something, not his death
or my own, but when I tell him he's a good dog
does it help? Does he get what a good dog he is?

I squat by him as he lies on his cushion,
just lies there as I stroke his fur,
as if he doesn't know I'm there
trying to tell him he is part of our lives.

When he was young, he'd look up if I just
thought of him, unfold from the couch
and come to me if I looked his way,
leap up all awag to my softest call.
Now I can't tell if he knows I'm here.

But when I stop stroking him, he lifts his head
and begins to lick my face (I let him)
with his big meaty warm tongue, licks
my nose, my lips (sealed tight), my cheeks,
passionately licks my nose, his eyes meeting mine
from way down that slender leather-tipped snout,

liquid eyes unblinking, as, telling me something,
he licks me and licks me.

🙞

We move sluggishly from room to room.
The dog prances before, after, around us
like a writer of corny romances,
punctuating our dullest lines
with exclamation points.

🙞

Conscientious dog! Kicking invisible dirt
over the mess she makes on the rug!

🙞

The old dog naps pressed against the front door. Getting in and out is an exercise in patience. Hearing, sight and smell all dulled, he's been caught napping in the living room too many times — rushed the door all bristle and bellow only to find the invaders chatting in the hall, hanging up their coats, amused at his fearsome worst, nothing to do but sniff their legs and give them token approval, as hangdog as a by-passed bureaucrat. He has been shamed too often. Now he sleeps smack against the door.

The old dog follows Pam now more closely than ever. He stumbles after her and she sometimes stumbles over him and shoos him away with a brief flare of pity and anger, but now she's getting something from our closet, as he trembles just outside on rickety shanks, looking off — gone into a dream. She comes out behind his back, starts to leave the room, reaches back to tap his

haunch. His head twitches alert, he stiffly turns himself
about and follows her, nose almost touching her thigh.

The dog has been old forever it seems.
Each time I buy dogfood I worry this will be
too much, he'll die, it will be wasted,
but each time he finishes every can and I must
buy more. Will it be like this for me, measuring
my days first in toothpaste and shampoo — trying
not to leave mid-container, then toilet-paper rolls,
then meals, taking smaller helpings in hopes of
making it to dessert, then not letting go of a hand,
lest from beside me yours reach mine too late?

&

Old friend, I hear
one of my years is seven of yours.
I'd slow for you if I could.

&

Each time I look at the dog
he's dead
in a new position.

&

The dog sleeps with slitted eyes —
dreaming? His eyeballs roll up and around
dizzily, patterns of white, then brown,
then brown and white, spinning past
the crescent windows until — a
noise . . . and JACKPOT!
Alertness overflows the eyes.

ஃ

CRACK! says the sky.
Eyes seek mine — two cats and two dogs.
They just look at me.

ஃ

Humanoid bodies can be so affectionate
and smart! Mine is almost
a real person — breaks its heart
if I leave it in bed and don't take it
with me on my dreams. But when it goes
(they're so frail), I don't know
if I'll get another one — such a
heartbreak to get attached to something
you have to put to sleep
after only 70 years.

ஃ

Someone in pain — my old dog — I can't help.
Hard to look on calmly. I feel compelled
to sympathize, be upset, lest calm evoke the keen
detachment of a professional torturer — and I
must have been one, his pain (or my inability
to ease or share it — or to get from his apathy
a recognition that I'm a good guy who wishes him
only well — or to impose my will on him, even if
only to get him to respond) IRKS me so.

I wanted him to sit still. He refused. Later I
wanted him to move. He refused. Now I want him.
He refuses.

"Have me killed," said my old dog. "PLEASE have
me killed!" I'm sure he said that — he must have.

An absence turns my eyes to open wounds.
Who pours this salt into my wounds?

Somewhere near grief it's very calm. Things
pass through or around me without rippling my
glassy surface. I am poised in pristine
transparency . . . but one twitch and the world
goes CRACK on all sides as I shatter into opacity,
so I hold very still, very calm, propped up
on all sides by the helpful solidity of air.

My dog is dead — he doesn't romp
Or creep or sprawl or nip or chomp —
But all that ended weeks before
I carried him through that last door —
And as I did, he licked my face . . .
I had to leave him in that place.
But in my head — or somewhere close —

He's with me yet: I feel his nose
Against my hand — he wants a pat,
And then another after that,
He wants my popcorn, begs for more,
Leaps up to join me at the door.

I've said goodbye, goodbye, my dear,
A thousand times — still, still a tear.

But if you say to darkness, "light",
What can the darkness say but "night",
And in reply, light simply glows,
The only answer that it knows,
Like you, old dog — you stubborn fellow,
Made of pure unalloyed HELLO.

After I have the dog put to sleep,
the dog cries all its tears
through my eyes, relieving me
of the mute, tearless gaze.

Good Good Doggie

My body takes good care of me:
I get shelter & affection & all the sensations
I can eat. Of course, at times I feel
a desire to get out; if I whine loudly
& scratch hard enough, my body realizes
I have to go & if not let out,
I may make a mess in the living room.
Then my body takes me out for a walk
on a leash.

Long ago my kind ran free in a wilderness
of stars, but now we are safe
& civilized, & if we run away
& are caught without a body,
we are impounded. The lucky ones
get new masters. Others are used
in experiments.

I am happy with my body.
When I am good & quiet & roll over
& play dead & fetch & shake hands,
my body will let me read a poem
or hear a symphony. If I stay
out of the way while my body makes love,
it lets me play with my friend

in the other body for a moment
before it falls asleep.

I am very good, & my body loves me.
It would not know what to do
without me. I am my body's best friend.
When it dies, the last to leave
of the mourners will be me,
whimpering by the grave.

Walking — I stop before a house to jot
down a poem, and some fool dog starts
barking, realizing I am about to
pilfer everything of value.

Growing Up Human

Another movie about someone's
"search for true sexual identity",
yet we give no attention
to those tragic beings who,
because they are in human bodies,
must conceal their really being
dogs. Imagine the agony
of having to sit quietly
and wait for the doorbell to ring when
with every eager bone and hair in your body
you want to rush to the door
and paw at it, yipping and wriggling
your behind! Imagine the embarrassment
when you nuzzle a stranger's crotch
and evoke a sexual response!
Imagine having to shake hands
and say "Pleased to meet you"
while repressing the urge
to sniff someone's behind!
Of having to eat vegetables,
having to kiss a girl or boy and remember
not to start passionately licking
the face — the difficulties are endless,
the pretense soul-blanching.

Of the 2.56% of Americans
who are estimated to be canian (or dog people),
even those few who "come out of the furnished
   rooms"
to live as dogs find life (in the words
of John Towser Pettibone)
"Rough! Rough! Rough!"

&?

The dog's twinkling four-step
flurries about my strong slow two-legged stride.
When angels walk with men,
will a hundred of our snip-snip baby steps
set off one SPROING of a seraph's
giant single foot?

&?

Sunlight absentmindedly strokes chairs,
table, floor, walls the cursory caresses
of a busy master with many good dogs.

&?

Tail Tale
(The Tell-Heart Tail)

Tail Tale is a poem written in hopes of fomenting a mass movement of millions demanding their full and just entailment, but, alas, the initial excitement drained away in the DE-tails of endless political debate over whether tails should be furnished to all of us by a government agency (the argument being that Federal Bureaucrats were THE experts on covering asses) or purchased privately by those who could afford them — and so the revolution fizzled, leaving behind (so to speak) nothing but the dream . . .

Tail Tale

Dogs hunt in packs, noisily stirring up game,
scaring it out of hiding into ambush.
They are clumsy stalkers, loud sneaks, lousy liars.
Hence their wagging, thrashing, thumping
joyfully idiotic tails, full of sound
and furry.

A cat's tail is a stalker's antenna,
slow serpentine, always controlled,
silently essing and caressing in passing
each tall blade of meadow grass.

Someday science will learn to say
from the thrust or waddle or wiggle
of our hips, from nerve traffic
at the tips of our spines — to tell,
had we tails, whether they'd catlike
coil or ardently wag or if some of us
would be of one sort, some another,
some using their tails as heavy clubs,
others to swing from branches, others
to rattle warnings, to swat flies,
to lean back upon and rest.

Or do our telltale eyes and tongues
say clearly what our tails would say?

If we had tails, would we wear them
in plain view? Would they protrude
from fashionable orifices in pants
and skirts? Naked? Or ringed, laced,
festooned according to sex, fad
and occasion? Or would they be sleeved
in wood, leather or silk? Or utterly
concealed, tucked down a generously
tailored trouser leg or among the struts
of a hoop skirt?

And if so, would one blush
if the hidden tail were stirred
to indecorous muffled motion?

Would children be taught to still
their tails, to drape them in a limp
stylized arch unknown elsewhere

in nature, trained to unleash them only
in most intimate settings, perhaps when greeting
lovers, parents, closest family and friends?
Would they learn a special tail flourish
for an older brother, another
for a younger, yet another for a sister . . . ?

Would we adults enjoy the little ones
running on the beach, still wagging
their untutored tails?
What would we do with revolving doors,
elevator doors, chairs, toilets,
quick-handed mashers on bus or metro?
What would medical insurance pay
for a lost or maimed tail?
Would we be able to teach our tails
to lie?

Would we envisage our spirits as tailed?
Angels with feathered tails? Tailed
constellations? Gods? Would we find statues
of Greek goddesses, armless and tailless?

Would women among themselves speculate
on whether the long or short of a man's
tail really signifies nothing? Would men
wonder if it's really better with a curly-tailed

woman? Would we dream
of sex partners able to do exotic
unspeakable things with kinky tails?

During public processions, would we
cross ourselves before or after touching
the Pope's tail?

Would Paris dictate the angle and style?
Would tails be "in" one season, "out"
the next? Would teen-agers get
tail-jobs? Bobs? At a glance
would we know rich from poor,
blueblood from nouveau, sophisticate
from boor by carriage of tails?

Would caudal therapy be all the rage?
"Release your repressions by learning
to thwhack your tail against the floor!"
("What an odd cult!" "Quite harmless.")

Would caudal come after oral and anal?
("Junior! Don't play with your tail!")
Would analysts argue our tails
more symbolic than real?

Would muscle men find ways to make
their sleek shaven greased tails bulge
like the gnarly boles of infected oaks?
Would sedentary tails draped over arms
of office chairs grow flabby, cellulite-
pocked? Would matrons do aerobic
tail-wags and tail-lifts to sprightly tunes
to regain the courage to show
their tails on a public beach? Would
spray-on undertail deodorant enlarge
the hole in the ozone? Would a business
pay you to walk down the street with a
banner hung from your tail to advertise
Joe's Bar or Call Monique! Would bannered tails
announce the advent of the world's end?

Would warriors of primitive peoples
collect the tails of slain enemies?
Of ancestors? Would we flock to museums
to see the preserved tails of Attila,
Napoleon, and Queen Victoria? (And
which tail would be huge and shaggy,
which as nude as a rat's, which trim
and prissy?)

How would tails and their twitches
transform our poetry? How many years
would Marvell set aside for adoring
his coy mistress' tail? If teeth
are pearls, lips cherries, eyes deep
pools, to what shall I compare thy tail?
To a firm, spicy sausage? A hairy
tongue? A stout treelimb? A vine?
A worm, eel, snake? (But these are no
comparisons, worms, eels, and snakes
being mostly tail.) To a slinky?
A stream? A whale's spume? A sinewy
smile? A banana? A pimple? A geyser?
(Haven't some of these been usurped
by our frontal tail?)

And what things shall find their
likenesses in our tails: "The meadows

swaying in the breeze like the tails
of a ballroom full of debutantes not yet
asked to dance". "Her smile, as formal
as a traffic cop's tail . . .". ". . . just
two shakes of a school marm's tail."

But tails perhaps receive as well as
send. The cat's delicate crooking
may be fine-tuning an antenna to carry
a signal from the grass or from wayfaring
incubi and succubi drifting up and down
the spiral staircase of an old house.
Perhaps, had we our proper tails,
our spines would find their proper length
to feed our brains signals
hitherto denied us by our abridged antennae.
Perhaps alien genetic engineers,
millennia ago, carved up our DNA
to trim the tails off our genetic stock,
lest we receive signals from the stars
to teach us how to leave this planet,
leave this galaxy, signals
to guide us home?

Or perhaps to spare us the horror
of knowing what is in each other's
minds. Or perhaps to enslave us

to our distrust of one another by hiding
from each other our noble hearts.

Or perhaps, when mammals stood erect,
the heavy-spirited among us slipped
out of our bodies and down our tails,
off the tips and away, leaving — like
empty shells strewn along the beach —
slumped bodies propped among trees
and boulders, until our alien doctors
helpfully slammed the trapdoors shut.

Perhaps it wasn't slipping: We habitual
haunters of heads would tiptoe down
the spiral staircases of our spines and
(disguised as bright pulses of energy)
escape out the tail. The DNA meddlers,
after shortening our tails, perhaps
bent under slightly each coccyx stub
so that any escape attempt would trigger
genital tingling, causing us to mistake

our yearning to be free of the body
for the urge to merge with another's,
conveniently producing more tailless
traps to tame more headstrong spirits.

Perhaps these same aliens planted ideas
in Darwin's mind to teach us that tails
were brute appendages we'd cast off
(and good riddance!) in our slouching
toward angelic erectitude. Perhaps . . .

No! No perhapses about it!
I'm sure that's the way it is!
Arise! Arise! You stubbed, snubbed, jammed,
less-than-human, maimed tailless pieces!
FIGHT the conspiracy to deprive us
of our hairy posterior heritage.
DEMAND TAILS NOW!

INDEX

A Crossing 34
A dog and a stick 29
A dog barks out back 23
A dog trots by 36
After I have the dog put to sleep 59
A Good Licking 14
A long walk with the dog 31
Another home 13
Another NO DOGS 29
As we walk away 15
As when walking the dog 22
At the house - the dogs 39
BAD body! BAD BAD body! 23
Bleeping motherbleeping bleep-sucking dumb dog! 50
"Can I pet your dog?" "Sure." 49
Carpe Canine 26
Cinderella 8
Conscientious dog! 53
Consummation 9
CRACK! says the sky 56
Curb Your Doggerel 16
Dog Days 23
Dog on Braided Rug 30
Dog on Braided Rug II 30
Dogs sweat through their tongues 20
Don't look at me that way, you dumb dog! 41
"Down, Tolstoy! Down" 29
Each time I look at the dog 55

Each with a white fluff of poodle	38
Far down the mountainside I see a tiny patch	44
From bathroom to bed . . . oops! Tripped	36
German Shepherd rages	22
Gold cocker spaniel looks at me from the lawn	44
"Good boy!" After 12 years	49
Good Good Doggie	60
Growing fatter	17
Growing Up Human	62
Halloween	44
Hard to express how much	41
Hard to sit on the grass	36
"Here's your food," I say	21
Hot, humid night	28
Humanoid bodies can be so affectionate	56
I, too, feel bad about the world dying	51
I walk past where the dog	49
I walk to the door	12
If this dog attacks	17
Ill-bred dog! I've never met you before	46
In Manhattan the people used to roam free	40
In the park, from a distance	20
Irish setter tiptoes	41
It is good to know	51
It must be breeding	39
"It's alright! It's a friend! Shhh!"	48
It's the beef-liver dog food.	50
Just for a second, he looked	21
L.A. night. Three stray dogs	39
Late autumn	12

Like Cats and Dogs 32
"Men" says the shrink "are animals." 38
My ability to love gets dried up 48
My dog is dead 58
My Good Dog 52
Old black dog 46
Old dog limps now 47
Old dog paces 46
Old dog romps 27
Old dog wanders off 25
Old friend, I hear 55
Old poodle can't see 33
Out of the pond 17
Physics Lesson 35
Polka-dots float in air 51
Poof! Snow-showered 21
Putting One's Best Foot In It 11
Riddle: Why did the dog cross the road 39
Someone in pain 57
Starting From Scratch 18
Sunlight absentmindedly strokes chairs 63
Tail Tale 65
The cats and dogs know 26
The dog beats her tail 20
The dog crawls up on the bed with me 47
The dog has had enough cuddling 8
The dog lopes ahead 12
The dog peers up at me, dabbing at air 41
The dog sleeps with slitted eyes 56
The dogs of third world countries 27

The dogs plop down on the floor	45
The dog sprawls on the couch	7
The dog stands still	47
The dog's twinkling four-step	63
The dog trots ahead	45
The dog, who leaves messages in urine	11
The old dog naps	54
The poet reads; outside a dog howls	19
The sign says "City Animal Shelter."	46
THUMP-pitpat THUMP-pitpat	46
"Tic . . . tic . . . tic . . ."	16
Tonight I move out.	29
Walking Beside You	42
Walking — I stop before a house to jot	61
Walking past	26
Wanted Distractions	28
We have cats, dogs and	40
We move sluggishly from room to room	53
We oversleep.	35
We take the dogs with us when we jog	24
When I've learned to feel joy	9
When the dogs crowd my knees	45
"Yip! Yip! Yip!"	40
You are not home yet	37
You Sly Dog, You!	13
You whimper at sight of another dog	10

About the author:

Dean Blehert lives with wife, Pam, and cat, Sally, (who does NOT go in for nose-licking, thank God, or Dean's nose would long since have been filed to a nub), in Reston, VA. He publishes his own poems in his poetry letter, *Deanotations* — to which a few hundred readers subscribe — and has had poems published in, among others, *Kansas Quarterly Review, Crosscurrents, Bogg, Visions, Lip Service, Gold Dust, Dark Horse, Modern Haiku, Carousel, Light, Orphic Lute, Brussel Sprouts, Stroker, Carousel, View From The Loft, The Listening Eye, HWUP* and *New York Quarterly*.

About the illustrator:

Pam Coulter Blehert, besides illustrating Dean's poems, is a fine artist (oil, acrylic, water color, etc.) who has won numerous prizes (including Best of Show) in local and national juried shows and is represented by several galleries nationwide.

ORDER YOUR COPIES NOW OF THESE PUBLICATIONS BY DEAN BLEHERT

Deanotations

A videotape of a poetry reading,
formatted by Warner Cable, 1/2 hour — $11.00
Shipping — +2.00

Deanotations Poetry 'Zine

Subscriptions — $10.00/1 yr
17.50/2 yr
25.00/3 yr
Lifetime — 100.00
Gift or student — 5.00/1 yr
All back issues (available - inquire for price)

"I read *Deanotations* the instant it hits my mail box."
- Marshall Cook, *Creativity Connection*

I Swear He Was Laughing: Poems About Dogs (Mostly) Who Only THINK They Are People

Words & Pictures Press, 84 pages, perfect bound — $8.95
Shipping — + 2.00

No Cats Have Been Injured or Mistreated During the Making of this Book: ...But Some of Them Are Disappointed — DEEPLY Disappointed — in Me

Words & Pictures Press, 84 pages, perfect bound — $8.95
Shipping — + 2.00

Poems for Adults and Other Children

Pogment Press, 64 pages, saddle-stitched. — $ 5.95
Shipping — +1.00

Dear Reader

Admiral Books, perfect bound — $3.00
Shipping — +1.00

The Naked Clowns

Great Western, perfect bound — $5.95
Shipping — +1.00

Available from:

**Words & Pictures Press, 18002 Irvine Blvd., Suite 200,
Tustin, CA, 92780, 714-544-7282, (fax) 714-544-7430.
CA residents add 7.75% sales tax.**